NORTH FOREST HIGH SCHOOL

W9-CGS-131

GETTING THE MESSAGE

Advertisements

Sean Connolly

A⁺

Smart Apple Media

Smart Apple Media
P.O. Box 3263
Mankato, MN 56002

Printed in the United States of America

Library of Congress Cataloging-in-Publication Data

Connolly, Sean, 1956-
  Advertisements / by Sean Connolly.
     p. cm. -- (Getting the message)
  Includes index.
  Summary: "Discusses the history of advertising and how businesses use advertising to targets consumers today, including print ads, TV ads, Internet ads, and viral marketing"-- Provided by publisher.
  ISBN 978-1-59920-345-4 (hardcover)
 1. Advertising--Juvenile literature. 2. Advertising and children--Juvenile literature. 3. Young consumers--Juvenile literature. I. Title.
  HF5829.C66 2010
  659.1--dc22
                         2008040702

Designed by Helen James
Edited by Mary-Jane Wilkins
Picture research by Su Alexander

Photograph acknowledgements
page 6 The Advertising Archive; 8 Mark L Stephenson/Corbis; 10 Bettmann/Corbis; 11 Hulton Deutsch Collection/Corbis; 12 Annebicque Bernard/Corbis Sygma; 15 Kieran Doherty/Reuters/Corbis; 16 NASA; 19 The Advertising Archive; 20 J A Giordano/Corbis SABA; 23 Tim Davis/Corbis; 24 The Advertising Archive; 26 The Kobal Collection/ Universal; 28 Gene Blevins/Corbis; 31 Axel Koester/Corbis; 32 Corbis; 35 Catherine Karnow/Corbis; 36 Jennie Woodcock; Refl ections Photolibrary/Corbis; 38 Jagadeesh/ Reuters/Corbis; 41 Heino Kalis/Reuters/Corbis; 42 Grove Pashley/Corbis
Front cover Mark L Stephenson/Corbis

9 8 7 6 5 4 3 2 1

Contents

The Power of Persuasion

The old car parked three doors down has a piece of paper in the rear window, with hand lettering: "For Sale: 80,000 miles: Offers above $1,000." Posters in the local supermarket spell out bargain prices for milk, bottled water, and chicken. Everyone at school is repeating the catchphrase from a television commercial selling breakfast cereal.

The miracle of love

A girl's joy, flowering like a rose, is radiant and full in the lovely miracle of love awakening. And for her a star, blazing bright as her dreams, will recall this moment always. Her engagement diamond, fair spark of eternity, reflects the light of her happiness in changeless splendor, and treasures its tender message of love until the end of time.

Remember, color, cutting and clarity, as well as carat weight, contribute to a diamond's beauty and value. A trusted jeweler is your best adviser. Extended payments can usually be arranged.

a diamond is forever

De Beers Consolidated Mines, Ltd.

The Message is King

Each of those examples is a type of advertising. And while people tend to think of advertising as being expensive and glossy—like the cereal commercial or full-page color ads in fashion or car magazines—the term describes a wide range of approaches.

What every advertisement shares with all the others, no matter how expensive or professionally produced, is the urge to communicate. The owner or maker of something wants to let people know about it. And then, having learned about it, people will

The De Beers diamond company found its luxury products hard to sell in the tough years of the 1940s. But its slogan "A diamond is forever" helped to turn diamonds into symbols of eternal love.

want to learn more or even buy the product or service. In other words, advertising is concerned with passing on information. Advertisers pay for the space (in a newspaper or magazine) or time (on the radio or television) to get their message across.

Most societies assume that advertising helps both manufacturers and buyers. Advertisers hope that the people at the receiving end of this information—readers, listeners, or viewers—will become buyers or consumers of what they are advertising. The producers of the advertised goods and services then earn back the money they spent on advertising (and they hope much more) through increased sales. This view believes that advertising informs the public and benefits those producing things.

Advertising can be defended in other ways. For example, the fashion magazine running lavish color ads can use some of the advertising money to produce its own glossy color photographs of the latest fashions. Without the ad money to pay for the color, the magazine would be forced either to run only black and white photos or to charge a lot more for each issue. Similarly, radio stations in many countries depend on advertising money to stay in business.

When Things Go Wrong

If all this sounds too good to be true, making it seem as though advertising makes the world go round—it is. Some people are misled by advertising that fails to tell the whole truth, or even tells untruths, about something. Others find themselves uncertain about where an informative news story in a newspaper or on television changes into a thinly-veiled advertisement.

The different media that use ads have guidelines and rules which govern advertising. But in a fast-changing world, people need to be aware of the fine line that divides persuading from misleading. The best advertising is lively, amusing, and ground-breaking. Consumers must be able to celebrate this while staying alert about the information they are receiving.

The Language of Advertising

Sellers have always tried to attract customers to try their products, whether they are stallholders yelling out the latest price of grapes, or banks running television commercials so that people will use their services. The way in which companies and individuals grab people's attention is called advertising.

The origin of the word advertising helps us understand how it works. The word comes from two Latin words—*ad*, meaning "to", and *vertere*, meaning "turn." So advertising is a way of turning people's attention

toward something (the product being advertised) and away from other products that might be competitors. Just attracting people's attention can make an enormous difference, tempting them to part with their money.

Today, no company can expect to survive without advertising. And because of that, the advertising industry is enormously important. Zenith Optimedia, a London-based marketing firm, estimates that companies spend about $412 billion around the world every year on advertising. This figure includes spending on all types of advertising—books, magazines, television, radio, and the Internet.

The Birth of an Industry

Advertising wasn't always such a money-making industry. When it began, it could hardly be called an industry at all. Despite the Latin roots of the word advertising, the ancient Romans (like other early civilizations) did not use what we would call advertising. Stalls and shops had signs showing what was being sold, and maybe where the goods came from.

In medieval Europe, towns and cities bought what they needed from local merchants and craftsmen. Butchers sold meat, wheelwrights made and repaired wagon wheels, tailors made clothing, and so on. If there was more than one of these merchants in a town, people chose one or the other because of their reputation. As the number of people who bought these goods and services was limited (because people rarely left their village or town), there was little reason to try to attract new customers.

Opposite: Bright and colorful signs cover most of the walls in the heart of Tokyo's central shopping district. Successful, eye-catching advertisements have helped Japan to become one of the world's leading trading nations.

Advertising as we know it began during the seventeenth century, as a direct result of one of the most important inventions in history—the printing press. New techniques had made it cheaper to print books and other documents. They also gave birth to newspapers, which helped to spread ideas and information across a city or a region on a regular basis. Merchants began paying for lines of text to appear in newspapers, as advertising. These early advertisements were what we now call classified advertising, which are simple descriptions of products and their prices.

New Products, New Techniques

The Industrial Revolution, which developed in Britain during the eighteenth century and spread to Europe and North America, changed the way things were advertised. Manufacturers began to produce more goods than local people could buy; their goods also cost less because they were mass-produced. So more people could afford to buy more things. As a result, the producers of goods began to advertise them, so new customers would buy them. Advertisements in newspapers and magazines became longer and more involved.

By the nineteenth century, advertising had become more sophisticated. For the first time, advertisers combined images with text describing a product and why people should buy it. Illustrated advertisements appeared as posters and were printed in newspapers and magazines. Advertising helped businesses to attract new customers and retain the loyalty of existing customers. However, companies could not afford departments to produce a wide range of advertisements. So specialty advertising companies, called agencies, developed during the late nineteenth and early twentieth centuries.

As well as producing advertisements for their clients, agencies spent money to find out about people's preferences and tastes. Understanding what people want—and how they would like to be told about it—became as important as informing people about a company's product. The advertising industry adapted to many changes during the

This late nineteenth century ad for a magic lantern (an early form of film projector) captures the excitement of an era when new products appeared on the market almost every day.

SPOTLIGHT ON
The Father of Modern Advertising

Thomas Barratt became a partner in the Pears soap company in London in 1865. The company's annual advertising budget was £80. Barratt created a series of catchy advertisements which helped the company grow enormously through the rest of the century. His campaigns included using the painting *Bubbles* by Sir John Everett Millais, which became the most famous poster in the country. He also persuaded famous people to recommend his soap as good for the skin. In 1897 he began publishing *Pears Shilling Cyclopaedia* every year. Many millions of copies have been sold and it is still in print today. Barratt eventually gained full control of the company, and increased spending on advertising to about £130,000. He believed that every penny was well spent because, as he stated more than once in public: "any fool can make soap; it takes a clever man to sell it."

Thomas Barratt used a popular painting by one of Britain's most famous painters as the heart of the Pears advertising strategy.

twentieth century. People soon became used to hearing advertisements on the radio and seeing them in movie theaters, on television, and on the Internet. Today, manufacturers no longer dominate the world of advertising. Modern agencies are experienced in getting the message across from what might have once been unlikely clients: governments, charities, political candidates, and even religious groups.

A Campaign Begins

Companies advertise themselves or their products for many reasons. A new company might be introducing itself to the public, and showing how it is different from competitors. A well established company might want to reach a new group, such as women or young people. Or it might be encouraging people to continue to buy its products or use its services. Advertising—getting a message across—is useful in all these situations.

Executives at Tokyo's Dentsu Advertising Agency check on the progress of advertisements for one of their clients —Salomon ski racing equipment.

Agencies and Markets

Companies and organizations rarely take on the job of advertising themselves. Instead they turn to specialty advertising companies, called agencies, to take on the job. Some advertising agencies are locally based, catering to large and small companies in a particular city or region. Others are huge companies which employ hundreds of people in offices around the world.

SPOTLIGHT ON
Inside an Agency

Major ad campaigns cost enormous amounts of money and involve hundreds of people. This is how most big advertising agencies are structured.

ACCOUNT MANAGERS

These people have the most responsibility and act as links between the client and the agency. They need to understand a client's needs and convey that information to the others in the agency. They also report back to the client on progress and present the finished product.

CREATIVES

This group of people does the thinking behind an advertisement campaign. Copywriters must fit their words to the visual ideas developed by art directors. Both groups need to understand both the client's wishes and the taste and opinion of the target audience.

STRATEGIC PLANNERS

These members of the team study different audiences and markets and then tell the creatives how to focus their message accurately and clearly.

MEDIA BUYERS

This important group deals with newspapers, magazines, television networks, and other media running advertisements. A successful media buyer can use influence to make a good deal for the agency (and therefore the client).

The link between the agency and its client (the company) is important, creating ties that can last for decades. For example, many observers believe that the contribution of the Saatchi & Saatchi advertising agency helped Britain's Conservative Party win a surprise victory in the 1979 general election. The governing Labour Party was expected to win, but unemployment was rising. Conservative advertisements showed long lines of sad, unemployed people over the slogan "Labour isn't working." Maurice Saatchi went on to become chairman of the Conservative Party from 2003 to 2005.

Staying on Message

A memorable slogan gives an important advantage, but an advertising agency needs to use it as part of a wider campaign. Deciding on how a campaign should work starts with discussions with the client, with frequent contact to make sure the agency's ideas stay close to the client's wishes. A campaign can last for a long time, aiming all the time to influence how people view the company and its products, so it is important to get things right.

A number of questions become crucial. First of all, what is the target audience? In other words, who will the advertisements be aimed at? Are these people young or old, rich or poor, male or female? For example, an advertisement for an expensive car will look different from one selling sneakers.

The agency and client then need to agree on what they want to say, how they want to say it—and how often. These issues relate to the language used in advertising (see pages 20–23), as well as the budget available. Huge companies spend millions of dollars over several years repeating similar slogans in newspaper and magazine ads, radio and television commercials, on the Internet, and on their own labels.

Some advertising campaigns aim to change the way people view the company or organization behind them. For example, during the 1970s and 1980s Britain's Labour Party became linked in many voters' opinion to strikes, inefficiency, and extreme political views. Tony Blair repackaged the Labour Party as New Labour just months after he became leader in 1994. The "new" was important as it put distance between his political ideas and those which voters linked to extremism and failure. New Labour went on to win the next three general elections—in 1997, 2001, and 2005.

Britain's former prime minister Tony Blair addresses the Labour Party conference in 2005. Blair helped the Labour Party to shed its old-fashioned image by renaming it New Labour and devising a new symbol—the red rose.

THE FUTURE UP IN SMOKE?

Imagine you are in charge of a new advertising agency that needs one big client to make money and establish itself. Company expenses are huge (renting offices, entertaining clients, paying employees, and so on), but income is low. You are contacted by a major tobacco company offering a five-year campaign advertising their top-selling cigarette. You disapprove of cigarettes and know several people who died as a result of smoking, but the company's future might depend on your decision. What would you do?

Over to YOU

Releasing the Message

Many of us buy items, such as movie tickets, drinks, or magazines, without thinking much about why we chose the way we did. An advertising expert might suggest that we had been persuaded that a movie was worth seeing, that one brand of soft drink tasted better than others, and that one magazine was more interesting than others on the shelf. All these decisions can be traced to successful advertising.

SPOTLIGHT ON

Advertising Space or Space Advertising?

Advertisers are constantly looking for new ways to display their work. Team uniforms advertise cell phones or computers, with hardly any mention of the team. Internet security systems promise to prevent unwanted pop-up ads from dominating computer screens. Ads are commonplace on the sides of buses or on theater programs. But in 1993, an American ad company proposed launching ads where no ad had been before—in space.

Space Marketing Inc., based in the state of Georgia, planned to launch 1 square mile (2.4 sq km) billboards in orbit around the Earth. Each one would look as large as a full moon. Mike Lawson, chief executive officer of Space Marketing, Inc., said that these space advertisements would be "a tremendous opportunity for a global-oriented company to have their logo and message seen by billions of people on a history-making, high profile advertising vehicle."

The plan produced protests in the United States and beyond. Astronomers and environmentalists joined forces with ordinary people who wanted the skies to remain pure. These protests helped the United States pass a law banning "obtrusive space advertising" in 2000.

Opposite: An American astronaut jokes about advertising a repaired satellite. Space advertising has become a reality as some countries have accepted advertising on their space vehicles to help fund their space programs.

People who do not work in advertising believe that advertising success is often the result of luck or genius—saying the right thing at the right time. The agency representing the De Beers diamond company came up with the slogan "A diamond is forever" in 1947; today it is part of the English language (and De Beers continues to profit from it).

The truth is that successful advertising is like inventor Thomas Edison's definition of genius: one percent inspiration and 99 percent perspiration. Agencies work long and hard to find the right images, words, audience, and outlets for their ad campaigns.

It might seem obvious to us now that diamonds do seem to last forever: they are one of the hardest natural objects and they appear indestructible. But in 1947, when many countries were finding times hard after the World War II, luxury goods such as diamonds seemed to be extravagances for many people—unless they felt that they were somehow buying a gift for future generations as well.

People need to be aware that advertisers try to create markets—groups of people who will buy the advertised products. The United States in 1947 probably had few millionaires thinking of buying diamonds. But it did have millions of hard-working people who were prepared to save or budget to afford some luxury in their lives. Advertising persuaded them to make that choice. Advertisers continue to persuade us hundreds of times a day.

TALKING HEADS

THE PREGNANT MAN

One of the most famous images of the twentieth century was an advertisement that showed a man in a sweater, looking unhappily at the camera while he rubbed his swollen belly. Below the photograph was the headline: "Would you be more careful if it was you that got pregnant?" The UK Health Education Council sponsored the advertisement as part of its drive to make men take more responsibility for contraception. Jeremy Sinclair of the Saatchi & Saatchi agency came up with the idea.

John Hegarty, who was the agency's deputy creative director at the time, had also been trying to come up with a startling image. When he saw an early version of Sinclair's idea, he was astounded: "I almost died. It was the best thing that I had ever seen. . . The pregnant man was more than just a piece of advertising; it was the first time that I had seen a piece of work that moved beyond the accepted boundaries our business operated in, commanding attention from a far wider group of people."

The message of the "pregnant man" advertisement gained enormous publicity for its client, the UK Health Education Council. The cleverness of the ad helped to turn Saatchi & Saatchi into one of the world's most successful advertising agencies.

Would you be more careful if it was you that got pregnant?

It's a lot easier for a man to have a baby than for a woman.
She's the one who has to hump it around for nine months.
She's the one who has to grin and bear it. Backache, morning sickness and all.
It's not a lot of fun being pregnant, if you don't want the baby. It's not a lot of fun being an unwanted baby, either.

The Health Education Council

Anyone married or single, can get advice on contraception, from their local family planning clinic.

Over to YOU

SETTING LIMITS

The United States banned obtrusive space advertising after a company proposed orbiting billboards. Can you think of somewhere else that should be kept free of advertising? Who should decide on such a ban? Who should enforce such laws?

New and Improved

The world of advertising has its own way of expressing things, almost as though advertisers use a different language. Fiction and poetry also use language in special ways; readers take pleasure in the way the writing style of a novel or poem reveals itself. But people approach literature in a very different way from the way they view advertising.

Readers choose what they want to read, and if they find the language difficult they can read more slowly or even re-read passages until they understand what they are reading. Advertisers know that they are up against a major disadvantage, which is that most people do not choose to read advertisements. Whether they flick past the ads in a color

supplement or change channels when a TV show has a commerical break, most people try to ignore advertising. The advertiser's job is to make people stop, look, and listen—and that takes special skills.

Understanding the Market

Advertisers constantly try to understand and influence the large number of people who might possibly buy a product—in other words, the market. They also know that people usually choose a product for one of two reasons:

• it is cheaper than others like it; or

• it is better than those of competitors.

Advertisements usually focus on just one of these benefits, and advertisers need to know which benefit is more important to their market. Not many people, for example, choose a champagne because it is the cheapest. Similarly, most buyers do not look for the best-quality paper clip—they are more likely to look for the cheapest.

Occasionally, companies can create a market and then sell these people the company's product. Think of all the different types of shampoo for sale. Some people might never have realized that they had split ends, dry hair, and dandruff all at once—until a shampoo commercial told them about this condition and what to buy to make it better. Changing an existing product so that it is "new and improved" can draw back customers who may have begun to wonder why they keep buying the product.

Hard Sell or Soft Sell?

Opposite: Pennants, flags, and offers of enormous savings in this New Jersey used-car sales lot are typical of the hard sell approach to advertising.

Having studied the market, the advertising agency and client need to decide the approach to adopt in a campaign. Should they bombard people with information, constantly repeating the product name and one or two of its advantages? Or should they create a pleasant atmosphere, luring the public into the ad in a way that links the product with that good feeling? These two approaches are known as the hard sell and the soft sell. A typical hard-sell advertisement in a newspaper might be one for a three-day sale at a local supermarket. The name of the supermarket is large and unmissable in the ad. The rest of the ad has eye-catching phrases such as "low, low prices," "while supplies last," and "unbeatable value."

Television and radio commercials sometimes use the hard-sell strategy. Think of commercials for leather sofas or computer equipment that seem to shout from the television. The hard sell is not subtle. And even if most people groan when they see or hear such advertising, the message sinks in often enough to encourage advertisers to use the approach again and again.

TALKING HEADS

DIFFERENT CULTURES

Experts and the general public alike agree that American advertising is often less funny and more concerned with the hard sell than the British version. Trying to work out why this is so, some people conclude that the reason lies in the media industries on either side of the Atlantic. Because the film-making and television industries in America are so much larger, it is easier for creative filmmakers to find work in those fields. In Britain, according to this argument, clever, witty filmmakers need to make commercials as a way of breaking into film or television.

Andrew ASC Ehrenberg, the former director of the Center for Marketing and Communications at the London Business School, takes a different view. He believes the difference lies in the way people in these countries view advertising: "There is a public view in the United States that advertising is a very powerful force, so the hard sell is more common there. Here, it is widely accepted that advertising is a very weak force and exists to reinforce existing attitudes rather than to persuade people of things they didn't believe before. That's why it tries to be so entertaining."

The soft sell approach, on the other hand, seems deliberately to ignore some of the unspoken rules of advertising. A printed ad of this type might show a happy couple or a group of friends enjoying each other's company. Visible in the ad, but not dominating it, will be the company logo. Soft-sell commercials also draw in people by linking a product with a sense of warmth or comfort. Puppies, for example, have very little to do with toilet paper, but many people associate toilet paper with a particular breed of cuddly dog (and buy that brand because of it).

What could be a softer sell ad campaign for toilet paper than one showing the cuddliest puppy viewers could imagine?

IMPROVED?

Try to think of five products that you have seen advertised as "new" or "improved"—or maybe both. Have you or your family bought more of them, or bought them more often, than before those words appeared on the labels or in advertisements? Do you think there are any real differences in these products?

Blurred Boundaries

Most people believe they can easily tell the difference between what is and what is not advertising. It is usually obvious which newspaper pages, or parts of a page, are advertising and which are not. In the same way, the commercial breaks during television programs are obviously advertisements.

THE FIRST AUSTRALIAN PERFUME.

Sheila

EAU DE PARFUM

(ALSO KILLS FLIES.)

But can we trust our judgement? Is it possible to be confused, and read or view an advertisement that we thought was a news story? The answer to the first question seems to be "not always" and to the second a troubling "yes."

The 1989 Sheila spoof advertising posters were so successful that many people tried to find sellers of the perfume—or insect-killer (see panel, right).

Grabbing People's Attention

In 1989, the London-based advertising company More O'Ferrall developed a new type of lightweight bus stop panel, which could display advertising posters. These panels aimed to attract the attention of people outside the stop—mainly motorists driving past—rather than the people waiting inside.

Some experts felt that drivers would pay no attention to these panels. So the people at More O'Ferrall came up with an unusual plan to win over the doubters: they advertised a fake product and promised that people would be talking about it within days. The product would not be advertised anywhere else, to test the effectiveness of the panels.

More O'Ferrall used 4,500 of their 30,000 panels around Britain to advertise Sheila. The ad showed a normal-looking perfume bottle, but with an outback-style hat instead of the usual lid. Next to it was the headline: "The First Australian Perfume." And in case anyone thought that this was a real product, a second line of text at the bottom read "Also kills flies."

By early April, people all over the country had begun to call radio stations, write letters to newspapers, and discuss this interesting new product. Ian Orsman, who was head of the cosmetics department at Harrods Department Store in London, said, "We've had requests coming in for it for the last week and a half. We found out that it was just an advertising stunt." The campaign might have been just a stunt, but it proved how effectively advertisers could catch the public's imagination.

Companies constantly try to disguise advertising so that people will believe that their claims that a product is better, cleaner, faster, or cheaper appear as fact. Some of these efforts are easy to spot. A late-night television program about the making of an album may be an infomercial which aims to boost sales of a pop star's new release. These shows are cheap to broadcast (as the record company has done all the shooting) and give a television station the chance to be linked to the pop star.

SPOTLIGHT ON
Product Placement

When we go to the movie theater, we expect to sit through a number of advertisements before the movie begins. But sometimes the advertising continues right through the movie itself. Movies cost many millions of dollars to make, so movie producers are always trying to find ways to raise money.

One method is called product placement. A movie producer approaches a company and says that a new movie could use that company's product (for example, a type of car, soda, or pet food) in some scenes. Movie-goers would see characters using these products, and the labels would be visible some of the time. In exchange, the company would pay the movie producers an agreed fee.

One of the most famous examples of product placement was in the film *E.T.*, made in 1982. Director Steven Spielberg's movie company, Amblin Productions, approached Mars Inc., the makers of M&M candies. They offered to show the movie's young characters luring the alien E.T. from his spaceship with M&Ms. In exchange, Mars would advertise the film on its candy packets. The company

refused, deciding that it did not want M&Ms associated with aliens from outer space. Spielberg's company then turned to the Hershey Company, which agreed that E.T. should nibble a Hershey candy called Reese's Pieces in a similar deal. The movie went on to break box-office records and sales of Reese's Pieces rose by 85 percent.

Other mixtures of fact and advertising are harder to distinguish. Newspapers and magazines often feature stories that seem—at first glance, and sometimes longer—to be news stories about the finest hotels or best cars. The typeface and headlines seem to be those used elsewhere in the publication. Only the words "advertising promotion" or "special report" offer a clue as to who has produced the article. Journalists describe these stories or reports as advertorials. The broadcasting equivalent is called an infomercial. It is easy to see how these terms arose.

Boundaries between advertisements and the real world can become blurred in unexpected ways. Many advertising campaigns rely on slogans or catchphrases that become popular with the public. Over the years, people have taken some of these to heart, giving a boost to the advertisers and their clients. Below are some of the most popular, some of which are still used, even if the company has dropped the slogan:
"Finger-lickin' good" (KFC restaurants);
"Melts in your mouth—not in your hands" (M&M candy);
"Just do it" (Nike sportswear);
"We try harder" (Avis car rental company).

LOCAL TEST

Free newspapers and magazines are delivered regularly to homes in most parts of the United States. These publications rely on advertising money, rather than sales of copies, to stay in business. Do you think these publications can be trusted to provide accurate information about some of the companies they review (such as hotels and restaurants), or do you think that the reviews are simply a front for paid advertising?

Targeting Youth

Young people are often described as tomorrow's leaders. Advertisers also realize that the young are tomorrow's buyers, so they devote a great deal of time and money to attracting their attention. At first glance, this strategy might seem hard to explain. Most young people have relatively little money to spend, so is youth-directed advertising something of a waste?

In fact, children are highly influenced by advertising and do their best to persuade their parents to buy their favorite products, as anyone who has been to a supermarket or toy store can confirm. Looked at in this light, children's advertising is really aimed at the adults who eventually pay for the products, with the children adding their voices to that of the advertisements.

But there is more to youth advertising than simply using children to influence their parents. Young people, like any customers, often build brand loyalty. If they start to wear a particular type of sneaker when they are young, they are likely to continue buying that brand in later life. Also, when they have more spending power, they might also buy other sportswear produced by the same company.

Opposite: McDonald's fast-food company has used the clown figure of Ronald McDonald to appeal to children since 1963. Some studies claim that he is the most recognized figure in the world after Santa Claus.

Governments, the general public, companies and advertising agencies need to find a balance between business freedom and responsibility towards children. Ads featuring or aimed at children generate sales and provide competition (both of which are vital to national economies), but they can easily take advantage of young people.

Becoming consumers

The UK communications watchdog Ofcom (see page 37) studies commercial TV closely, especially the way in which children are exposed to—and come to understand—television advertising. Their research points to the following pattern of development.

- Most children younger than four or five view advertising simply as entertainment and make little or no connection with the product.
- Between the ages of four and seven, children begin to distinguish between ordinary shows and advertising.
- By the age of eight, most children realize that commercials are trying to persuade them to do or buy something.
- When children enter their teens they begin to engage with the content of commercials. They listen to the message and decide whether or not they are persuaded.

Because younger children are less concerned with the details of a commercial message, advertisers make ads at a level at which children can become involved. That means using bright colors, lively music, animation, and cartoon characters. This type of advertising is hardly the best preparation for developing a critical sense, as it aims to hide any message beneath the entertainment.

TALKING HEADS

INTERNET ADVERTISING

A 2006 report found that eight of the top ten food brands that target children in TV ads also use web sites to market to children. The web sites offer chances to spend unlimited time interacting with specific brands in personal ways.

"Online advertising's reach isn't as broad as that of television, but it's much deeper," said Vicky Rideout, director of Kaiser's Program for the Study of Entertainment Media and Health, who oversaw the research.

Over to YOU

STERNER LIMITS?

Children's advertising comes under stricter controls every year in developed countries. Television advertisers are told what and how they can advertise at times when children are watching. Yet many of the problems that advertising controls try to guard against—such as childhood obesity resulting from eating too much junk food—continue to increase. Do you think the answer is to ban all advertising from children's television?

SPOTLIGHT ON
The Power of the Internet

Young people are not simply targets for skilled advertisers out for a profit. With their technology skills, they are often the first to use new forms of communication to their advantage. An excellent case in point is the "Yes We Can" video that swept the Internet in early 2008.

"Yes We Can" is a highly successful example of viral advertising (see page 40), supporting the American presidential candidate Barack Obama. Much of Obama's support comes from young people, who echo his calls for sweeping change in the way politics operates. Obama supporters display posters with the slogan "Yes We Can," referring to the chanting that often accompanies his speeches.

Hip hop artist Will.i.am (right) took four and a half minutes of an Obama speech and composed a song to accompany the candidate's words. He and other Obama supporters—including Scarlett Johansson, John Legend, Aisha Tyler, Nick Cannon and Amber Valletta—sang or recited parts of the speech, returning again and again to the repeated phrase "yes we can."

The "Yes We Can" video shows how the Internet can be an immediate—and cheap —way to advertise. Will.i.am thought of it on January 29 and had it finished and uploaded to the YouTube video site by February 2. It has been viewed millions of times on the site, and at one point was getting a million hits a day.

Going Too Far?

The advertising industry constantly finds itself in the midst of controversy. Sometimes being controversial can be helpful: some advertisers might cite the old saying that there is no such thing as bad publicity. An extreme example of someone who held this view is P.T. Barnum, the nineteeth century American showman. He once said of his critics: "I don't care what they say about me as long as they spell my name right."

As a rule, advertisers know they must take care not to turn public opinion against them or the products they advertise. In the age of instant communication a consumer backlash can spread quickly—through e-mail, text messaging, and community web sites. If a company or advertiser is caught behaving in an unethical way, the bad publicity may last years.

How Far Is Too Far?

If P.T. Barnum's view of publicity is true, then why should advertisers and their clients care about what people think? After all, advertisers are paid to get people's attention and—if all goes well—to keep it. If there is something a little naughty or edgy in doing just that, then who can really complain?

Opposite: American showman P.T. Barnum was proud of the weird and exotic exhibits he displayed. For years, the main circus attraction was Jumbo, the largest elephant on Earth. Even after Jumbo's death in 1885, Barnum used the elephant's skeleton to attract customers.

The answer is that companies keep a close eye on the people who make up their market. If even a part of that group—people wearing glasses, curly-haired children, dog lovers—feel offended by an advertisement, then those people might choose to buy a rival product. And if they feel strongly enough, they might mount effective public campaigns against the company or its product.

Advertising thrives in countries that have a strong tradition of free speech, so it can be difficult to impose legal restrictions on what can or cannot be said in an advertisement. People with complaints can use some of the same legal actions that apply to any print or broadcasting. For example, a company can be taken to court if an advertisement contains a libel or if it encourages illegal behavior. If an advertisement makes a dishonest claim about a product—for example, how effective a diet pill might be—the agency or parent company could also face legal action.

SPOTLIGHT ON
The Marlboro Man

Fifty-one-year-old Wayne McLaren died of lung cancer in Newport Beach, California in 1992. During his last years, McLaren had been an anti-smoking campaigner. His cancer almost certainly developed because of the 25 years he was a regular smoker. McLaren's death was not so unusual —about four million people die every year as a result of smoking-related illness.

What made McLaren's death noteworthy was his past. Many people remember him as the Marlboro Man, who featured in advertisements for Marlboro cigarettes. At first, the cigarettes were marketed for women. But, from the early 1950s, advertisements showed the Marlboro Man—usually a cowboy or hunter—smoking a Marlboro cigarette.

Wayne McLaren was one of many different men who were used as models for the Marlboro Man. The advertising campaign was familiar around the world, which is why McLaren's illness and death received so much publicity. McLaren spent much of his last year campaigning against cigarettes—and especially against tobacco advertising. One of the last things he said was: "Take care of the children. Tobacco will kill you, and I am living proof of it."

The Social Cost

Most advertising steers away from being illegal. But that might not be enough to keep advertisers in the clear. The reputation of a company can be damaged if some of its advertising claims are proved legally to be false. But a company could find itself with a steeper uphill battle if its advertising is linked to attitudes that society frowns on.

Today, few agencies would produce advertisements of the sort that were common in the 1980s. Many ads at that time appeared to promote an aggressive, win-at-all-costs attitude to life. Likewise, modern consumers are offended by ads that seem to reinforce racial or gender stereotypes. Concerns about social justice, religious freedom,

and the environment lie behind many people's reaction to advertising nowadays. There is little chance of an advertiser being charged with supporting environmentally wasteful behavior. But people will make up their own minds about supporting such a company.

The Marlboro Man advertisements aimed to generate new sales by linking the cigarette with the rugged men of America's West.

Over to YOU

PROTEST LIST
See if you can list five advertisements (from television, magazines, or the Internet) that you consider misleading or offensive. Ask a friend to do the same and then exchange lists. Was any ad on both lists? Did you find that you and your friend agreed on what counted as "going too far"?

Advertising Watchdogs

If a family paid an electrician to rewire their house and the wiring led to a damaging house fire, they would probably take the electrician to court. They had a legal agreement with the electrician to pay for a job done well and to recognized safety standards. Similarly, a driver would expect some sort of compensation from a garage if a wheel they had replaced fell off at high speed.

The consumers in the cases above would have known that professional organizations set standards for electricians, car mechanics, and many other trades. Members of these organizations must meet these standards in all their work: otherwise they might be taken to court or punished in some other way.

Who Is to Blame?

The advertising industry must also be prepared to face criticism and complaints from the public. Misleading, demeaning, and false advertising can stir up trouble from the very groups the advertising is targeting (see pages 32–35).

Advertising restrictions aim to keep alcohol, tobacco, and other dangerous substances away from young people.

The question is, who is responsible for advertisements: the companies advertising the products or the agencies they employ? The advertising industry, in the United States and in many other countries, recognizes that the government could draft and enforce strict regulations if it does not take responsibility for its work. This recognition led to the creation of the National Advertising Division (NAD) of the Council of Better Business Bureaus (BBB) in the United States, the Advertising Standards Authority (ASA) in the United Kingdom, and to similar bodies in other countries.

Consumers can complain directly to the NAD or ASA, which examine the complaint and reach a decision on whether it has merit. The argument against this system of self-regulation is that complaints can only be made, and offensive advertising stopped, after an offense has occurred.

The Broadest Coverage

The NAD, ASA, and groups like it also act as watchdogs in monitoring companies which produce advertising that comes under government control. For example, tobacco advertising is banned in many areas, alcohol advertising is strictly controlled, and children's advertising constantly faces new regulations.

Organizations that act as advertising watchdogs often work in partnership with other groups dealing with wider broadcasting issues. In the UK, for example, the Ofcom watchdog oversees broadcasting on radio and television. Some of that broadcasting is advertising, so Ofcom acts alongside the ASA in keeping the industry fair and respectable.

Over to YOU

DOES THE SYSTEM WORK?

Do you think that a system of advertising self-regulation works or should the government do more to control advertising? What are the arguments for and against any change to the system?

The Final Analysis

In 1957, the American journalist and social critic
Vance Packard published *The Hidden Persuaders*, a book
which examined the advertising industry. Until then,
Americans had accepted advertising as a fact of life,
something that—like the weather—was always
around but that they could not do anything about.

Packard turned his attention to many things we now accept, but
which seemed revolutionary at the time. Without overloading his
book with statistics and footnotes, he gave people an insight into how
the advertising industry works. Some of what Packard wrote

has dated over the past 50 or so years. For example, he appeared to think that housewives could be almost hypnotized by some sorts of advertising. He did, however, open people's eyes to how the industry worked and how advertising affects people generally. In that respect, Packard's contribution has been enormous. Nowadays, some people spend their entire careers analysing advertising. Even more importantly, consumers have become far more aware of how advertising works—and many have used this knowledge to their own advantage.

Clued In

Twenty-first century consumers are far more aware of the media than their counterparts in the 1950s. Advertising finds its way into nearly every area of the media—from traditional newspaper classifieds to cold-calling telephone advertising to web pop-ups and banners to viral marketing (see page 40).

Opposite: Huge call centers in India provide countries in the English-speaking world with a pool of capable workers who can deal with telephone business. They are linked to those countries via modern communications systems. Call centers also enable advertisers to use cold-calling techniques, phoning people at home to sell them products or services.

Today people—and especially young people—are bombarded by advertisements throughout their lives. These can be heeded or ignored if people have the skills to identify the advertising for what it is. Some people may be especially vulnerable to these increasingly sophisticated attempts to influence their behavior, especially young and very old people. Governments often try to build safeguards into commercial deals, so that fewer people suffer as a result of being misled. For example, many financial contracts (for purchases, insurance, or investments) have "cooling off" periods during which buyers have a chance to seek advice if they feel they were rushed into a deal, or if they were misled.

Other young people, on the other hand, have shown that they can turn the system on its head. By using the same technology and communications developments that helped advertising evolve (especially cell phones and the Internet) they can send out alternative messages—for social change, against the power of big companies, or simply to publicize themselves and their projects.

SPOTLIGHT ON
Viral Advertising

Experts on advertising and marketing are always on the lookout for new trends. One of the most successful recent forms of promoting ideas—known as viral marketing or viral advertising—combines new technology and old-fashioned word of mouth. People spread the word about a movie, book, band, or album by text message, e-mail, or on social web sites. Viral advertising has two main advantages. It taps into modern communication technology, so it can target thousands of people instantly and at low cost. Links to the web and cell phone networks help to give viral advertising its edgy, up-to-the-minute feel. This is what prompts people to forward viral ads on to their friends.

Some of the most successful examples ignored traditional advertising strategies altogether. *The Blair Witch Project*, a low-budget horror film, became incredibly popular after its release in 1999 because news and clips from it were released on the web. Made for $36,000, the film has gone on to earn nearly $254 million.

The Arctic Monkeys, a band from Sheffield, UK, also used viral marketing to become popular. The band approved of fans who uploaded versions of their songs on to community web sites. More than 140 versions of some Arctic Monkeys songs were on the web—and the band was selling out concert venues—before the first official single was released in 2005. The Arctic Monkeys have gone on to become one of Britain's most popular bands, headlining at the Glastonbury Festival and winning several awards.

Almost two-thirds of the web sites quoted in the Kaiser Family Foundation study (see page 30) used viral techniques. Children were encouraged to e-mail their friends about a product or invite them to visit the company's web site. For example, at juicyfruit.com, users were encouraged to "Send a friend this fruitylicious site!" and told that if they "send this site to five friends" they would get a code to access additional features on the site. Other sites encouraged young users to send friends an "e-card" featuring the company's brand or characters. For example, on Keebler's Hollow Tree web site, children are invited to send a friend some "Elfin Magic" in a birthday or seasonal greeting.

The Arctic Monkeys were a top band on the Glastonbury Pyramid Stage in 2007, only two years after they released their first single.

DESIGN AN AD CAMPAIGN

Try to think of how you might advertise a new type of running shoe, a charity helping blind people, a pop festival, a new flavor of ice cream, and an environmentally friendly car. Which type of advertising would you use for each campaign? Could you use a similar technique for all of them? What factors would influence the type of advertising you would choose?

The Shape of the Future

What is the future of advertising in this Internet age? The 1982 sci-fi movie *Blade Runner* was set in 2019 and offered a bleak view of an overcrowded Earth, with menacing lifelike robots, skies darkened by pollution, and advertising everywhere—including on airships floating above the city.

This is a disturbing extension of the idea of advertising in space (see page 16). The filmmakers intended audiences to feel uncomfortable about a world dominated by advertising. Some of the developments the movie portrayed are already happening: do they offer consumers more freedom or less privacy?

Advertisers are always trying to reach their target audience at the least cost. Thousands of people every day see the giant billboards in New York's Times Square or London's Piccadilly Circus. Even the sci-fi airship advertising of

Advertisers might try to reach the youth market by sending advertisements to cell phones. Phone users receiving the ads would be charged less for calls and texts.

Blade Runner might soon be a reality. The problem with this type of advertising is that it is expensive and that its content is not automatically noticed by people walking by every day.

This is why many advertisers are looking to a future where "less is more." By focusing on a smaller group—but knowing that these people will actually see the ads—advertising companies can cut costs and achieve a higher success rate. Techniques being developed today signal how the advertising industry could look in 10 or 20 years.

Organizations already track the ways in which people use the Internet, passing on information to companies that fit the same profile. If someone, for example, spends a lot of time looking at sports web sites, he or she might begin receiving e-mails or seeing pop-up ads from companies which make sneakers, sports equipment, or sell tickets to popular sporting events.

A Fair Deal?

Other companies are beginning to offer advertising as a way of helping consumers to cut costs or to afford new technology. Cell phone companies already offer deals that slash phone charges—as long as the customer is willing to receive ads broadcast over the phone. These deals are targeted mainly at young phone users, who have less money to spend.

The American company Accenture has found another way to weave advertising into the fabric of people's lives. It is developing technology to help people turn their digital photos into slide shows that can appear on screens anywhere in the house. The catch? The same software enables Accenture to slip advertising into some of the family photos.

As always, advertising continues to bewitch and offer glimpses of worlds that people want to visit. In the past, people have been able to control what they were presented with—by flipping a page or by changing the channel on the television. Will people still have that freedom in the future?

Glossary

advertorial   A newspaper advertisement that looks like a normal news story.

agency   A company that produces advertising.

brand loyalty   Buying a particular make of product again and again.

classified advertising   Small newspaper or magazine advertisements, usually just a few lines of text.

cold-calling   Phoning strangers to advertise something.

consumer   Someone who buys things.

critical   Relating to the skill of judging the real meaning (of, for example, advertisements).

demeaning   Portraying individuals or a group of people in a negative way.

developed countries   Richer countries whose people have more money to spend.

engage   To respond to something with full understanding.

environmentalist   Someone who supports efforts to protect the Earth.

extravagance   An unnecessary luxury item.

free speech   The freedom to speak freely without censorship or limitation.

glossy   Expensively produced.

Industrial Revolution   A period which began in Britain in the 1700s, when goods began to be manufactured in factories rather than by hand.

infomercial   A radio or television advertisement that resembles a normal program.

investment   A way of using money in the hope of making more money.

libel   An untruth about a person that is printed in a publication.

logo   The visual symbol of a company.

mass-produced   Manufactured in large numbers by machine, rather than by hand.

media   The different forms of mass communication, including print, radio, and television.

obtrusive   Unwanted and obvious.

orbit   A circular path around a planet.

self-regulating   Not relying on the government to impose controls and restrictions.

stereotype   An oversimplified and often biased depiction of a group of people.

unemployment   Being without a job.

unethical   Deliberately wrong.

World War II   The war that lasted from 1939 to 1945 in which Germany, Japan, Italy, and their allies fought the United States, the UK, China, and their allies.

Further Reading

Advertising and Marketing. Careers in Focus. New York: Ferguson, 2008.

Gifford, Clive. *Advertising & Marketing: Developing the Marketplace.* Chicago: Heinemann Library, 2006.

Standford, Eleanor, ed. *Advertising.* Introducing Issues with Opposing Viewpoints. San Diego: Greenhaven Press, 2007.

Web Sites

I Buy Different

http://www.ibuydifferent.org/

Just Think

http://www.justthink.org/about

National Advertising Review Council

http://www.narcpartners.org/

Teen Consumer Scrap Book

http://www.atg.wa.gov/teenconsumer/

Index

	DATE DUE	

10030000936273

659.1
Con

Connolly, Sean
Advertisements

$23.95

DATE DUE	BORROWER'S NAME

10030000936273

659.1
Con

Connolly, Sean
Advertisements

$23.95

North Forest HS